FUGITIVE

❋

FUGITIVE

✺

CHRISTOPHER NELSON

NEW MICHIGAN PRESS

TUCSON, ARIZONA

NEW MICHIGAN PRESS
DEPT OF ENGLISH, P. O. BOX 210067
UNIVERSITY OF ARIZONA
TUCSON, AZ 85721-0067

<http://newmichiganpress.com>

Orders and queries to <nmp@thediagram.com>.

Copyright © 2024 by Christopher Nelson. All rights reserved.

ISBN 978-1-934832-94-3. FIRST PRINTING.

Design by Ander Monson.

Cover image by Sayan Ghosh.

CONTENTS

On Self   1
Certainty   2
Melancholia   3
Memory   4
Fugitive   6
Titration   8
God   9
Theology   11
Eden   12
Union   13
Blue Flags   14
Lethe   16
Mind   17
Cancer   18
On Night   19
Baseball   23
Innocence   24
Desire   25
Dereliction   27
Chaos   28
Frost Asters   30

Acknowledgments   33

ON SELF

for the cancered cell that I also am
forever selfward with the tenacity of sickness
for forward now forward then when perennially retreating
for why else bring a razorblade to the dance
fortnight after fortnight the lusts declined
for I busied myself against the silence
for the pumpkins left to rot
for this we bowed for this we did no
for the caterpillars in first frost
forestalled and beaconless
forty something years before we learned
fortune may it forever evade you
for sure—
for the silvered maples we claimed were dancing
for what I ran from with sapping regret
for what I ran from
for what I thought nightly in bounty
for what isn't discernable from self
for you always
for we went where darkness coaxed
for why else would it or would we
for the bereft of—
for the windmill in the stillness

CERTAINTY

One inch beneath the surface the roots
make a kind of net, which I break

so I can put you in, royal catchfly, so I might
attend to your growing—given rain, given light,

luck, and, most difficult, my constancy—
so I might look up from the dishes or

daydreaming and be a little stunned by
your shock of red, as on a walk we come across

the aftereffects of a fistfight. And maybe, with
more summers, you'll be established, and the

hummingbirds will duel for your nectar so we
can mistake it all for a dance—

a few more summers, which we should have.

MELANCHOLIA

Staring into the orchard for no reason other than
to stare. September light and the detritus
that's blown in against the ancient pear
that bears hard fruits I feel terrible
about letting rot. Seven years since you let
inside your head the patient bullet.
A detail I come back to: an open book beside you,
two-thirds read, some fantasy—dragons, witchery,
the promise of escape typical of the genre. Earlier this year
I pulled a patch of scarlet gaura, mistaking them
for horseweed. Only one survived: backlit, hundreds
of pink-white blooms small as spiders suspended
on stems thin enough in this late hour to be invisible.
As kids we huffed gas in a meadow from a red tank
woodcutters left behind. When everything shimmered we
ran, but I couldn't feel my body, my legs
just something churning below me, and me
somewhere far off, watching. The gaura lives one year,
maybe two, a fact that is for some reason
unbearable tonight. We dropped acid and climbed
your roof to watch the stars. We spooked when
you said, "They're watching back." The fantasy
novel, mid-chapter—and the fact that it took
a month for anyone to find you. Folklore says
horse thieves used to rub their hands
with gaura blooms to calm the animals—
come to in the night by unknown men
talking softly and moving slowly, as if yielding to
a caution already renounced.

MEMORY

I think we called it
Bonner's Hill or Bonner's Mile
because it seemed that long
and he used to live there
though he died by the time we were
old enough for the dirt bikes we
pedaled to maximum speed
before the tuck and float all
the way down helmetless
dodging potholes and loose gravel
at the riverbend
where they found
the city girl no one knew
in a pink fur vest
her head crushed in
we'd coast at the bottom for
a whole song on the Walkman
after blasting through
the intersection of third south
a four-way stop arms out
like the just
crucified
still ablaze with
indignation
or like one liberated from
a cell that became a second mother

womb-dark and scarce
of life-milk
scrounged from the end
of cocks and dreams
dreams where she visited
where the dace and tadpoles flickered
in a brook so clear you could
drink it from cupped hands
you could lave it over
an infant's mouth without fear
who was it
dared the hill in blindfold
Eric or Derek or Jacob DeLain
before their dad moved them for
a factory job injecting plastics
no, it was the train
before his dad fell asleep
on the rails, before the long howl
and whatever it brings

FUGITIVE

The eastern cousin of wild bergamot isn't
native to our region, but enough have escaped
from gardens to make their presence common,

yellow and purple like the stuffed harlequin clown
of my kindergarten. When as kids we watched
on the copter cam OJ's white Bronco clear

the interstate, I knew TV would never be
the same. How we touched tongues once
during a sleepover. How your parents

encouraged us to shower together to save water.
How the water when we washed Dad's Pontiac
for bowling money flushed to the gutter with a

head of foam, but the birds drank it anyway.
When he sold the car and neglected to remove
the plates, the police called at 3 a.m.

because it had been used to rob a pharmacy.
How it's never fully dark in jail. Always
the permanent fluorescence. Sleeping faces

in "safety light." I watch my son sleep in the rose
night light, time already galloping
away with him, a mare capable and opaque,

more machine than promise.
How dry its muzzle. How large the nostrils
that flex and blow.

TITRATION

Late enough into the year that the after-
work walk is nearly dark, pale orange
horizon behind the supermarket.
Trees leafless and the non sequitur hum
of the final lawnmower, someone still committed to
a front yard shorn as a putting green for
neighborhood dogs to shit on and semi-
domesticated raccoons to lumber across
at midnight to unlock a suet cage or unlid
a compost bin for a shard of pumpkin or
handful of cucumber peels. The calendar-perfect
crescent moon still able to bewitch my
imagination and surface memories: how I
watched you sleep—we were sixteen for one night—
naked in moon- or streetlight blueing your
lean, hairless body. How I allow the sight
to come in formally like a respected
but frightening visitor. How once we carefully
divided a square of paper smaller than a pinky nail
—blue lightning LSD—the summer they killed
Roy Dunsmore, summer of fireflies,
in a hay field beside Interstate 15.

GOD

I wish I liked sparrows more,
drab, profligate invaders from England,
and we all know that You watch them,
and how You watch them is with my eyes
and the eyes of the neighborhood cats and other
sparrows and cardinals and the caddisfly with its 300 eyes,
and You able only (maybe?)
to take it all in. When I moved here, in some
ritual need to belong, I picked two colanders
of white clover flowers (introduced, like me, naturalized,
potentially invasive, creeping perennial)
and made of them a yucky pioneer pudding,
the recipe from some local newspaper forty years old.
Dumped it after two nights of choking it down,
disgust replacing my enthusiasm for authenticity.
The little league field back home was full of white clover,
preteens crushing their lambent millions
under hand-me-down cleats.
After one game my best friend's dad
punched the ump in the throat. When the coughing man
regained composure he asked for
a witness, and my dad said he didn't see
a goddamn thing. I sat in the clover
by the parked Buick watching sparrows eat
smashed bugs from the grill, flutter and bite,
the scissor beaks clicking sometimes if you listened,

if you ignored the madness and pain of fathers.
In winter they stick around, can wipe out
a whole feeder of sunflower and millet in a day
—and they're short days—and then shiver all night
to keep warm—and they're long nights—only to
repeat it for four or five months. Cold enough, easy,
to kill you when the snow plows fail and
you're stuck in the shoulder watching the red needle
dip toward the fateful E. I thought of You then,
the night we got thirty inches, trembling,
the little engine behaving all Your laws,
especially the one about endings, You looking out
at all the glistening and finding, despite my
panic, reason to keep on.

THEOLOGY

said the blade to the lamb we're in this together

said the garden to the god when do we have a say

said the lamb in return yes but only one of us is an exit

said the poet to the moon none or few but you & you O you

said the god to the garden I give you locusts and you give me your

yearning said the moon in reply why

said the sayer to the said we bled with a pity unique to men

said the men in chorus know you not the principle of the knot

the one that binds & the one that gives

said the garden to the man without me you're just another animal

said the animal to the god we know you like the smell of water

said the water the only word, house & seed of all others

the unspliced root, the mother even of god who sets down

the gavel & astrolabe to try a hand at gardening

to be green again after so much silence

so much noise in the code

EDEN

Picking apples from the seven old trees—
six since the spring ice storm—trees we've neglected,
twigs and branches jutting vertical and downward.
Two wheelbarrows full, and three times that
on the ground that we've let rot and squish
under foot and attract wasps
ants, gnats, butterflies, beetles, and all manner
of life I can't name. From the playpen, our son
sings, screams, cries, sings again,
waving the toy ukulele like a flaming towel
before settling down to try carefulness
and the single pluck. Early fall, a break in the rain,
the groundhog has taken over the woodshed again,
the bats the crawlspace. Asters, so many blooms
they're collapsing, purple as mythology,
purple as the robe on the picture-book Jesus.
In my future when (as the house painters and
carpenters say) a man past 40 starts to fall
from ladders, that future, when my backwards
descent shows me the fatigueless blue sky
then my upside-down house, then my wife,
her twelve-foot apple fork aloft, lost
to ancient industry and song. When I land
in the fetid mush, may the bees not scatter,
may their feast continue, may they care
nothing of me, may they keep the truer way.

UNION

I was kissing you when the dog bit our son's face and the snow us and flourishing and the rain in perfect blue-gold columns and you said yes and I said yes and we said nothing and we went into the lake like a Hollywood and held as the headlights shot up and trapped the squall surprised us and the orchard buds were slick with ice and the lump I found when emerged the miniature doom already in tragedy and we snow fell away and the shoulder nothing nothing nothing nothing nothing

BLUE FLAGS

A meadow in May, driving home from
their first camp together, the lovers, still
pungent from each other, stop

to take them in, walk out among them
in the boggy ground, their papery and delicate
blooms unavoidably signifying

celebration, never mind their poisonous root,
which centuries ago herbalists employed for
syphilis and strangeness

of the gallbladder and had their own names for
though most agreed to call it *fleur
de Louis*, after the king, but we know

what becomes of kings, so they called it
fleur de luce, but we know the implications of
praising light, so they called it *fleur

de lys*, and it stuck because no one knew what
it meant, which seemed appropriate for a
flower of such beauty, for what really

can beauty ever mean? The lovers
are kneeling beside them, getting muddy,
as if the whole show is for them,

which it is—that's the first purpose
of desire, its bridge the color between
spirit and matter. Also named after

the god's messenger, Iris, who brought
to us fleeting beings words of the divine,
and harkening to the iris of the eye,

small circle of the body's wildest color
and the pupil in the middle, the portal
that opens and opens in the presence

of the lover, and not even in their absence
can it close. She has a handful of them, emblems
of no country but kingdom without boundary.

LETHE

nor will you at field edge, fog
    flanked and frightened, fully
    forget your wonder

nor will I ever not wonder what
    we might have been or become
    or bore, mulelike, motherwise

into the birthsky of first vision,
    and should that solemn silence
    give, as in cease, or break open into

the language before words, before we were
    worlds or were worlded into
    these small forgettable things,

next time, could there be such
    a promise or premise,
    I will slip from the gray raft,

fog over water, water immediately, horribly
    cold, a cold without a dram of
    mercy, just to be there

    with you
    as you go down

MIND

Before you shot yourself in the chest, I had forgotten you.
Visiting here after 25 years, false claimant of homeland,

I'm pocketing columbine seeds from the library garden.
How like me to make this about me. Your mother

in the grocery store moving slow and hunched among
the frozen dinners. The joker you dated in high school—

was I wrong to see in you limitless potential?
But then we're all beaten by something. How the methadone

was too expensive after the heroin, which was too cheap
to refuse after the Vicodin, which was too necessary after

the accident—seven metal pins along your spine,
which was a lovely spine, the spine of a swimmer,

your muscled willowy-ness occupying an entire province
in my mind. How an idea becomes a kingdom. How even

imagination can't keep the castle from being sacked.
Catapult bombs, flaming turrets. One black cross

-bow bolt from the murder hole crashes
the escape carriage. Valiant may we be against ideation.

CANCER

For years Father knew he carried
    a timebomb
he could never set down
    and not even
the specialists could say when

I watch him lean toward the mirror
    and behold
a pink sore with an attention
    and tenderness
reserved for his prize-winning roses

In the good summer dusk
    they compete
with the sunset's two
    million colors
only a fraction of which are named

ON NIGHT

> *—a cluster of peonies is called a ruin*

What is better than ruin
for the soul (that soldier) who
on a lie he recognized as such said
I will go forth
                into the fire ceaseless?

Even death (the theory goes)
has existence because of you— *You*—
                        so why not

give up
            already
give over
            the gold—the goal
give it back to You
            the soul
            my soul—*this* soul

(language feeble
       tool
     we fashioned
    or found or
  were given / granted
              fails us now)

Now I'm dreaming him again—funny, Father, how you sneak in—
1972, and how many clicks from Saigon?
    where the hooker children offer
    their backsides for the price

              of a milkshake and burger—

night (shadow of flame) and you / he / my memory

(which are You, again, always)
            puts the needle where
            the blood river flows

from the poppy which bears its own ruin
(another flower that begins with P and ends
            with *why*)

so that he can be
    so stoned he can't be-
lieve the situation is real:

to lead them, these men—young—that he's come to know,
into the booby-trapped
        jungle
        sweeping right left right
        the metal detector

                              no wonder you spent the
                              remainder of your months
                                                silent

jump forward—the medium
        allows us
        this pleasure / this necessity—

48 calendars later
        you're so dead I can
                tell people
                and feel nothing

I do think though
        that you'd be proud
        of mine
        my ruin
        this hedge of them
        pink, bulbous and full
        as tits or
        grenades

I love that they let me be—
no water, no weeding, just
sit back and trust the sap
                to flow

             ask the ants who work
                          as if
    night, when it comes, won't
    end   as if
                       soldiers
                       of God

the word comes from Old French
and means "one who serves
in the army for pay"

                  further back
     the Latin *solidus*, the name of
                    a solid coin
                    not one thinly plated

but go forth, soldier / soul, into
                       what?

                  some place
                    to place
                  attention
                     intentions

how an ant at dawn
             maws
           a globe
           of dew

BASEBALL

when the catcher
tagged the sliding runner
at the plate but took
a cleated foot to the nuts

Father cradled his head
like a mother or lover
then helped him stand and
walked him slowly to

the shadowed pavilion
and gingerly removed
the pin-striped pants and
jock strap to see

and held his hand as
he winced and allowed
him to feel the degree
of swelling both nearly

weeping now and I but
a schoolboy with a
schoolboy's understanding
watched for the fissure

where manhood had sneaked
the june bugs delirious
in the halogens above

INNOCENCE

That's what the pioneers called the blooms—
small, delicate, weak, lavender on the outer edge,
glowing in the center. That time of year
when snow probably won't come again. I had to
remove the rubber bands from my braces
for your cock to fit in, and I gagged
when you reflexively tried for deeper.
There, it's said. It's good to get certain things
out of the way. But you were *a way*, and I
a pilgrim carrying such frail powers as
promise, belief, and the uncertain sanctity of
my body, which I barely understood, how
it could open and tremble and flush. Usually
annuals—one season to show off then one
of sorrow and rot—some can be frail
perennials, coming again to the body confident
with experience, empowered to claim
their one now. We called them bluets
and picked each one in sight, pressed them
in an anthology between Ibsen's pages.
Next year, as in allegory, we return
to the site of bounty and come away empty.

DESIRE

The motherwort's won
one-third of the field, and the heavy

late summer bees so vigorously
work its openings that the acreage seems

beset by its own wind.

As tall as me, some taller, the odd
blossoms adorn a central stem,

not the normal fingering bracts.
Since sixteen I've vaguely wanted

to die. There, a confession, buried

like a cancerous cyst, in the very center.
Some of the early bloomers—black-eyed

Susan, purple coneflower, coreopsis—
have sent up desperate reminders,

more glorious in their strident

yellows and punctuating magenta,
now that they rise from

or are tangled among
those withered and waiting for fire.

I mean, if it isn't in you, you're done for.

It wasn't my intent but I lied: not the very
center but a bit askew, there is a door

concealed by vines—small, yet even
a grown man could crawl through

in a spasm of daring.

DERELICTION

Random beside a barn or the lone one
in a tulip bed, two, bright as children's
clothes, beneath a fence row, another
in a concrete curb crack, and more
among the panicled grass, invisible until
blooming, hidden like spies or herpes,
only goodness, the pure pink goodness that,
in its time, decides, yes, to open and
let inside the tongues in their wild varieties
and singular hunger. Phlox. The name means
fire, a softly haired fire, given to eruption,
the quiet kind, the kind we wake from and
continue into, continuing in its perennial
stunning, we come away only to come back.

CHAOS

The hottest day of the year, we rest
in the shade of black walnuts. I'd put off
re-shingling the west side of the barn
after a straightline wind handled the heavy asphalt
sheets, strew them like playing cards. Wet from
humidity we share a lemonade,
flecks of shingle gravel stuck to our arms,
your cheek, under my nails. I take from you
a salt kiss, thankful shingles were all we lost.
The mistflowers, little purple pompoms, dot
the shadows at the property's wild edge,
a small woods, nearly all walnut, whose
juglone poison kills most plants unlike them,
invisible battle in the soil, easy to mistake
the effect for leaf rust or wasting disease.
The neighbor spreads walnuts on his driveway
then rolls his pickup over them. Later in the week
he will bring a loaf of bread, apologizing
for the poor quality, but it will be delicious,
moist, umber, the flavor of earth. When I climb
again the barn roof with three nails between
my lips, the sun is lower but the shingles
still burn my feet through my shoes,
and the wasps I'd startled up have settled,
and from here I'm higher than the bird cherry, and
I see you in the garden, moving heavily, pregnant

over seven months, beside a growing pile of weeds,
becoming someone we don't yet know.
Three nails for the last new shingle,
darker than the others—sun bleached,
a little soft, one good wind from tearing free.

FROST ASTERS

I mentioned them before but
failed to convey how pervasive

how remarkable a million white blooms
small as children's fingernails, a million

in an acre and you
in the old coat walking

your evening constitutional, sleet or sun
wind or dark, the pastel meadow

the overlooked miracle, the third
child turning inside you, its still lightless

ocean, its unutterable potential
its unfathomable fragility, the white

wave the purple foam, such is
the evening bearing down, its gentle

thought, no song no prayer no
way, its perfect non-negotiable

embrace as you near the bend where
I won't be able to see you with my eyes

and the lights click on at the marked hour
and the owl in the orchard makes known

its place for the other
who comes in this life and the next

ACKNOWLEDGMENTS

I am grateful to the editors of the following publications where some of these poems previously appeared:

Blossom as the Cliffrose: Mormon Legacies and the Beckoning Wild: "Blue Flags," "Eden"
Cherry Tree: "Innocence"
Cincinnati Review: "Memory," "Mind"
Fairy Tale Review: "Theology"
Foglifter: "Desire"
On the Sea Wall: "Fugitive"
Poetry East: "Cancer," "On Self"
Poetry Northwest: "Melancholia"
RHINO: "Certainty," "On Night," "Union"
Seneca Review: "Chaos"
Sixth Finch: "Titration"
Sporklet: "Dereliction"
The Windhover: "God"

CHRISTOPHER NELSON is the author of *Blood Aria* (University of Wisconsin Press, 2021) and four chapbooks, including *Blue House*, winner of a Poetry Society of America Fellowship. The recipient of the 2023–24 Amy Lowell Traveling Scholarship, he is the founding editor of Green Linden Press, a nonprofit publisher dedicated to poetic excellence and reforestation. His anthology *Essential Voices: Poetry of Iran and Its Diaspora* received a Midwest Book Award and was named one of the best poetry books of the year by *Entropy* Magazine. Visit CHRISTOPHERNELSON.INFO.

❈

COLOPHON

Text is set in a digital version of Jenson, designed by Robert Slimbach in 1996, and based on the work of punchcutter, printer, and publisher Nicolas Jenson. The titles here are in Futura, which is the best font for titles. Come at us, haters.

❊

NEW MICHIGAN PRESS, based in Tucson, Arizona, prints poetry and prose chapbooks, especially work that transcends traditional genre. Together with DIAGRAM, NMP sponsors a yearly chapbook competition.

DIAGRAM, a journal of text, art, and schematic, is published bimonthly at THEDIAGRAM.COM. Periodic print anthologies are available from the New Michigan Press at NEWMICHIGANPRESS.COM.

Printed in the USA
CPSIA information can be obtained
at www.ICGtesting.com
JSHW021248140124
55353JS00003B/94